STONES IN THE WATER
BY
KENN AMDAHL

Stones in the Water

Copyright 2015
By Kenn Amdahl

ISBN-10: 0692331271
ISBN-13: 978-0692331279

All rights reserved. No part of this book may be reproduced in any way, including written versions, electronic versions, audio versions or by any other means whether or not invented or in common use at the time of this publication without the express written permission of the author and publisher. This book may not be scanned, converted to PDF, EPuB, mobi or other electronic formats without the express written permission of the author and publisher. Unauthorized reproduction is expressly forbidden regardless of the reproducer's compensation, including distribution for little or compensation. Even free copies are forbidden.

Anyone who encourages or assists in distribution unauthorized versions by downloading such versions, bypassing copy protections systems, or by creating or hosting a website that provides unauthorized downloads, or provides links to websites that do, shall be considered an accomplice to the theft of intellectual property and liable for damages including punitive damages to the full extent of the law.

Anyone who downloads, gives, or receives unauthorized copies of this book, or any book, is also an accomplice to the theft of intellectual property. Beyond that, they are stealing the livelihood from authors, artists and musicians and condemning future generations to a bland world where there is no incentive for creative people to strive to improve and bring joy to the world by their efforts. In that world, powerful corporations and dull committees will control all forms of entertainment even more than they do today. Is that what you really want? Thank you.

Clearwater Publishing
P.O. Box 778
Broomfield, CO 80038-0778

ClearwaterPublishing.com

Other books by Kenn Amdahl:

Fiction:

The Land of Debris and the Home of Alfredo

Jumper and the Bones

Nonfiction:

Algebra Unplugged (with Jim Loats, Ph.D.)

Calculus for Cats (with Jim Loats, Ph.D.)

There Are No Electrons: Electronics for Earthlings

Revenge of the Pond Scum: Searching for the causes of Amyotrophic Lateral Sclerosis (ALS), Alzheimer's Disease, and Parkinson's Disease

Joy Writing: Discover and Develop Your Creative Voice

Essays:

The Wordguise Alembic Volume One

About this book

I've been writing words on scraps of paper since third grade. Some grew into novels, nonfiction books, or songs; others morphed into articles, blog posts, or stories. Some never evolved. They remain orphan words on envelopes and shopping lists stashed in cardboard boxes in my basement. This book is what a few of them look like, all typed up.

As to the book's title: Years ago, a friend was leaving on some exotic vacation. At the time, I was too broke to travel. On an impulse, I asked him to throw a stone into those distant waters on my behalf. He did, and it made me feel good, almost as if I'd traveled there myself. "Throw a stone into the water for me" became one of my little mantras. Kind friends and strangers have thrown stones into various bodies of water on my behalf all over the world. Some have given me photos of the act, as if I required proof. One friend, visiting Manhattan, had access to neither stones nor bodies of water so she threw some ice cubes into a cocktail on my behalf. It seemed to work just fine. Another, leaving a big city, realized he'd forgotten to throw a stone. He made the taxi stop on a busy bridge so he could throw some pennies over the side for me. He didn't exactly understand the game, he said, but he hoped that worked. Hundreds of stones, pennies, and ice cubes imbued with some tiny part of me lie quietly at the bottom of pristine mountain ponds, frozen glacial lakes, filthy rivers near bright colored temples, and steaming swamps. A Real Poet threw one in the River Thames for me. I wish I'd kept a journal of my pebbles.

Thanks to my family, friends, and strangers for all the stones, real and metaphorical.

Special thanks to people who published some of these poems; I apologize for my fragmentary records. Back when I was actively mailing poems out into the world, I became obsessed with collecting rejections as if they were stamps or butterflies. Acceptances were nice, of course, but not really part of the collection; they did not merit a special file or notebook. I even submitted poems to journals with interesting names just to get a rejection from them for my collection. It's not as easy at it sounds. I coveted a rejection from Exquisite Corpse, for example, as if it were a one cent British Guiana stamp from 1856; alas, they merely sent back a yellow Post-it note with the single word "sorry." That did not seem sporting at all.

I have credited the first publishers, as well as I remember them, at the end of this book. I've thrown a stone into interesting waters on behalf of each of them, especially those I fail to mention. I hope that's good enough.

Contents

Almost Thirty-Nine	9
The Dying Buffalo	10
A Tiger is Coming	12
The Oldest House in The United States	13
La Rodentia	14
Something You Don't Want to Do	15
The Weapons of Joy	16
A Mutt in Alaska	18
Italian Food	19
With a Little Help	20
Silk	22
Five	23
The Deer	24
The Journal	25
Rain	26
Genesis	27
Wyoming	28
Lonely Skin	29
Fowlplay	30
Camping	31
Big Sadness	32
Tadpoles	33
The Condor	34
Koo Lack a Lack	35
The Dance	36
Dissolving	37
The Guitarist	38
Rudolph's Dad	40
Practice	41
April Sleet and Monkey Eyes	42
Dry land Farmer	43
Bar Talk	44
Little Khomeini	45
Warm Water Friends	46
The Waterfall	47
Underground	48
Illusions	49
The Leader	50
Growing Up	52
Brain	53
Tonight	54
The Dark Horse	55
Time Flies	56

Modern Love Song	57
Old Pets	58
Trees	59
Rituals	60
small fish	61
The Night I Learned Jon Killed Himself	62
The Boy Who Loved Thunder	63
Good-bye, Richard	64
Met Before?	65
Mary M.	66
Ironsides	68
A Gray Painting	69
From a well	70
Fall	71
Makeup Queen	72
By a New Mexican Road	73
Jim the Handyman	74
Secrets	75
Sailor's Song	76
Near a Colorado Ghost Town	77
Good Places	78
The Stone	79
Yesterday	80
The Valuables	81
August	82
Postcards	83
The Dull Sonnet	84
Ghost Writer	85
Along Roads	86
Collecting	87
Frying Chains	88
Raw Wheat	89
When Ocean Met Lava	90
Y2K	92
The Grizzly	93
re: A.E.	94
Terminal	95
Gammon Dace	96
Smoke Signals	102
The Weed	103
Fruit	104
Cheap Transportation	105
Sharpening Stone	106
Acknowledgements	107

Almost Thirty-Nine

Write me a poem without breasts,
Leave out the seasons, ice and growing things,
Remove the scented paint, the dazzling sound,
The crash of music, the soft skinned brute,
The bleak loneliness.

Speak simply and without tricks;
Save us both the magician's embarrassment:
The empty hat.
I close my eyes and wait.
Write me a poem without cutting edges,
Water, darkness or light.
Give me something I can grasp
When senses leave my body
Like bats from a cave at dusk;
Give my thirsty lips a sip
Of that soothing, tasteless fluid:
The poetry that remains
When the poem is removed.

The Dying Buffalo

The tired old head of the dying buffalo
Lay in pooled moonlight near the corner of the zoo pen.
His cheek-bone hard against the dirt, like an Indian, listening,
Each ragged breath blew clouds of dust
From red infected nostrils;
Pus and blood oozed from his open mouth
And flies attacked his eyes.
The ancient gods gave one small gift:
The night-guard had a girl with him,
And wine, and plans; the office lights were dim...
The old one would have peace enough to die.

Yellow eyes flickered, and the buffalo traveled,
Uncaged of time and walls, as buffalo always do
The evening of their death.
He stood beneath a street lamp now,
Amid suburban lawns and sidewalks
And houses made of fog, as if unreal,
Phantom houses, phantom streets,
A dim disturbance on his immortal prairie.
He pawed the earth, young again and regal,
Breathing in the sagebrush magic,
Breathing out white frost against the stars,
Traveling back in time, the houses fading...

A car horn honked, he shuddered...
Once again he wheezed within the squalid cage
Too tired for life, or dreams. A woman's young laughter
Floated from the guard's office.
The breeze moved stiff brown hair,
His eyes closed, and he was running, running,
His hooves pounded dust from the ancient homeland,
Now laced with ghost-like roads and cars,
That slowly disappeared.

A million buffalo beside him crushed the memory of the future
Into clouds and thunder against the blue sky.
No horse or man or time-devil could contain
This rolling pride forever.
This was the time that was no dream,
When God was a herd the size of clouds,
And man watched, fearful, from pitiful safety
And the buffalo feared no mortal thing.

The night moved quickly; such nights do.
A tilt, a shift, the stars spiraled,
The sleeping earth changed position...
He stood among others, much older,
That no longer looked like buffalo;
Huge beasts, as he was now huge,
At the edge of an ocean
That would soon dry to prairie.
The sky was full of lightning and magic,
Shadow herds, the size of clouds,
Raced above the waves, flickering and unreal,
Phantom animals, his history, and his future.
The others, the old ones, stared at the ghosts on the water
And pawed the ground, as if to say
Join us...
It is time to begin again.

A Tiger is Coming

A tiger is coming, I don't know his name,
But he moves like a shadow at dusk,
He waits with the sure eyes of death for his claim,
In the stillness of spice trees and musk.

A tiger is coming, I've not seen his face,
But I've heard the grass sigh in his wake,
There is no philosophy in his cold eyes,
And his fangs leave no room for mistake.

The tiger who comes, I can't say who he loves,
But he whispers a name to the moon,
His muscles ripple like silk when he turns,
Yes, a tiger is coming here soon.

Kenn Amdahl

The Oldest House in The United States

The old, old house in Santa Fe,
Tourist attraction, adobe cocoon,
A two-room cave, we enter from the gift shop,
Graffiti on the walls older than me
Older than my father;
Bones and sticks that haven't moved for centuries.
I sneeze dust that a Spanish missionary
Sneezed half a millennium ago,
Dust that was once an Indian hunter,
Dust that was once his antelope prey.

I linger in the cool inner room
All shadow and silence.
Through the tiny arched door I see my wife and children,
Already in the anteroom,
On their way back to Thursday morning,
Bored at plain adobe,
Bored at mere ancientness
Dutifully they inspect graffiti;
No one notices I have not followed them back out.
One by one they file out the passageway.
I want to call out, with a joke about being deserted,
But something stops me.
Is this what death will be, I wonder,
As perfect silence wraps around me,
As the last of my sons turns, finally, wordlessly away
To rejoin the noise and lights of the world,
As the coolness holds me motionless
As the dust welcomes me.

La Rodentia

Rats have lovers, too,
Panting, rolling in the muck and ooze,
The scent of sewage clinging to her matted fur
As sweet to him as Juliet's perfume.
Rancid meat clings to pointed yellow teeth:
An aphrodisiac as strong as football shoulders,
Gentle words, or a fine new car.
Her shiny, wet reptilian tail:
A low-cut gown of lace and silk.
His quick red eyes: a sharply tailored suit, and Redford's smile.
The piles of rotting cabbage, corn, a small dead bird
Within his stinking hole:
A wallet full of crisp new bills, a condo in Vail,
And new furniture.
Her claws, oozing scars and chewed leather ears:
A long and shapely leg, in sheer stockings and white high heels.
Their shrieks and squeals and whining chatter:
Soft and lovely jazz, Michael Franks, perhaps,
On the stereo, in the candlelight,
Where the love is made.

Kenn Amdahl

Something You Don't Want to Do

Is this: When your pet tarantula dies
And you see him through the aquarium glass,
Legs curled beneath him, perhaps upside down,
And you finally get brave enough to take the lid
Off, and reach in and touch the tiny hairs
And stroke the soft brown back,
Finally even lifting the carcass out of its cage,
Placing it prominently on your bedside table
For shock value, feather light and harmless.
As if to prove you never were afraid, really,
You leave the lid off the aquarium,
Promising to clean it tomorrow. You'll take out the sand,
The water dish, the box he hid in.
A dozen times you wondered if he had somehow
Magically escaped, but no. Each time he was only
Hiding in his little box.
Now he's escaped, you think,
Turning out the light. You remember his skill
At walking up the glass, testing the lid
For weakness. His carcass, not so far from your face
Makes you nervous, but you know you're being silly.
And you go to sleep.

A few hours later you wake up.
The room is very dark and something is nagging at
Your mind. Something you
Read once, perhaps. You turn on the light. The
Empty shell of spider has not moved.
This bothers you, but you know you must do it. You grasp
A tiny leg and snap it off.
It's hollow. No juice, no meat.
No spider.
You had forgotten that tarantulas shed their skin
A perfect, hollow replica of themselves.

The Weapons of Joy

                An exuberance of dazzle
             Ambushed sleepy earth this morning,
        Sucker-punched gritty-eyed late sleepers;
Flashing light slapped the ticklish moving lake,
Coaxed a giggle of leaping, falling rainbows
From the cool, sensual water;
Poised and paused,
Then, with a shimmer,
Cast off the disguise of familiarity,
Stepped from the perfect hiding place of everywhere,
       And stood there, naked and grinning.
            "These are the weapons of joy," the lake laughed,
"The secret spinning engines of happiness," the light answered.
"Soaring swelling glee to fill your throat,
       Impossible reunions, glistening iridescence,
            Smile and song and laughter — the weapons of joy;
                 What coldness in this
            Or any world
Could resist them?"

My friends pity my lack of religion
And make me visit the books and dark buildings
Where their God resides.
They console me with candles, prayers, and incense
In rooms where passive brown leaves
Wait for the winter that turns them to dust,
Hoping they are not leaves, after all
But seeds.
Desperately hoping Spring will find them;
Constructing eternity,
Seriously following the tedious instruction book,
Step by step
By step.

Kenn Amdahl

But I sang with my God this morning,
    Loudly, laughingly, and carelessly off-pitch,
      As children sing, and madmen,
   Drunk with delight at simplicity
 Armed with the weapons of joy;
I've been infected with the dazzle, and contagious,
    For I am earth, stirred together by music,
  And my god is Sunlight
Dancing with Water.

A Mutt in Alaska

Easy friends, like huskies,
Show up periodically,
Bark a happy greeting,
Rub against your leg,
Then go lay down,
Content in the corner.
You can sustain a lot of these.

But the pup who needs attention,
Who must be petted,
Must be fed, let out, then in,
Is a burden.

You saw me wag my tail,
And scratch a muddy paw against your door,
Obviously useless for pulling sleds,
And your face said dog-pound.

Italian Food

She chooses their pizza,
He doesn't care. Sausage or extra cheese,
Even onion; Insignificant details compared
To the glow of being with her.
She picks the movie,
He nods. Fine. Anything's fine.
Movie, no movie, a blank screen;
Just smile once;
Let me be near your warmth.
She schedules their dates,
Between her meetings, her job,
Her obligations, commitments, and other entanglements;
He rearranges his calendar. It is
Nothing. A tiny price to pay.
Not even a price.
She decides what their relationship will be,
And he is startled.
She does not pause, but makes the necessary
Adjustments to her life,
Content and pleased,
Until she realizes, with a vague sense of confusion,
She is eating her pizza alone.

With a Little Help

I want a hit of that Joni Mitchell drug
Straight and raw, whatever it is,
The stuff she grows in blue motel rooms
And candle-lit cafes, somewhere in Europe,
Far away from fame, yet close enough
To feel its icy loneliness
Her dealer sells rivers to skate away on,
And the clouds of Michelangelo,
She hides her stash in a room full of secret pastels
And antique mirrors.
My dealer sells puns.
I want the number of her pharmacist,
And an open account.

I also want a long slow pull
On the bottle Gordon Lightfoot hid away;
I'm certain a rainy day friend would share it.
We'd watch all the ladies in their finery
Dancing like rainbow trout in the country evening,
He and I, wooden sailboats that long to be gone
And yearn to stay. We'd walk with dreams
That understand men
But dissolve like the weather girl
Leaving only a scent and a memory
And we'd reach once more for the bottle...
Yes, let me be drunk like that, just once.

I need the disguise Paul Simon has rented,
And, of course, his dictionary.
Let me bundle up, safe and warm,
And throw snowballs at the crowd,
Make everyone duck, except the children,
And the other well-bundled people.
There but for my lack of grace, go I.

A few drops of Bruce Springsteen
And I could cut back on my coffee.
A shot of Hoyt Axton Tequila and I won't feel so bad
When women confuse me.

While we're at it, order me a bag of
Claudia Schmidt's magic powder;
I'll wake up all alone, deep in the night,
Hear the rain, and not be sad, but smile.
Or step on broken glass,
And wish a former lover well.
Peter Pan could use such dust.

Fill my bag, if I've any currency left,
With a few gems that might not fit in everyone's earrings:
The Bob Lind rubies, the Fred Engleberg sapphires,
Stanley Jordan's right hand, a well-worn Paul Stookey or two,
The Roches on Tuesday nights, draped over my shoulder,
And a baseball cap that says "The Bobs."

I'll feel dressed as fine as Ricardo Montalbaum, selling cars,
I'll fly, wild-eyed and bat-like over cities and prairies
With a grin on my face and a buzz in my head
To make the Texas Chain Saw Assassin jealous.

Silk

He filled the page with words,
Then ripped away the excess
Until all that remained was this:
    A scarf of deep blue silk
    Danced on the window sill,
    Fingered by a breeze.

The scraps of paper on the floor said this:
    I ache to touch your skin,
    I cannot bear the sadness
    Of being without you,
    I wake dreaming that I taste your mouth...

He filled another page,
Built a massive tree of words,
Then chipped and whittled
The twig that remained might have been
An antelope, listening to the rustle of leaves.

The scraps near his chair said
    Death would be smaller
    Than this loneliness.
    But for the pain it would cause you,
    I would nestle there tonight.

He lit the scraps;
The flames his dignity,
The soot his privacy,
The smoke his life,
And left behind blue silk, falling
And the rustle of leaves.

Kenn Amdahl

Five

My life has escaped.
Hours have oozed out of it,
Minutes have fluttered into the night;
My mind was a cage
Whose bars were too far apart.

The Deer

My headlights caught a deer,
Sprawled lifeless on the twisting road
As if transported from some famous work.
The fog pulled back, surprised, for just a moment,
And gave my brakes time to save me
From the instinctive deadly swerve
Where there was not road enough to swerve,
Between the cliff and icy river.
My heart snare-drummed, breath
Hissed from me in rapid clouds
As I stumbled on stage in the twin spotlights of my car,
Thanking the god I believe in
For the miracle of my survival.
I rolled the lifeless meat toward the black water
To save the next unsuspecting driver,
And then I saw the belly move.
An unborn fawn still lived inside;
I thought of the hunting knife in the trunk
And of the appointment that would not wait,
And of the cold, cold water.
With my hand on the still-warm belly
I stared at my own headlights
Alone with the fog
In a stolen play that no one
Will ever see.

The Journal

I am the pages in her journal
She will one day rip and burn,
Wistfully, but resolutely.
There will be no tears.
The surprised flame will lick a corner,
Tentatively at first,
Then awaken, hungry and intense
To its small rage.
Her hand, hovering safe above,
Will feel once more
The heat of skin barely touching,
Skin that must touch skin,
The consuming lust,
The drunken pull toward each other,
The depth of eyes
Searching lover's eyes.
Everything that no one knows
Will curl and blacken;
The smoke, the heat, the memories,
Finally dissipating.

Rain

No rain for the old woman-
Wait, not so old;
But skin like paper, wrinkled, shrunk
Around her bones,
Eyes too large, staring;
Hunger works faster than years
To squeeze the juice from a woman.
She lies in a spot of hot shade,
In some distant land,
I see her in my mind.
But the shade no longer matters.
The flies that land upon her mouth
No longer matter;
Let them lay their eggs.
Too hard to raise the hand
Or shake the head and make them fly
No time for rain to work, even if it came.
Only time to wait a little longer

It's January in Colorado;
I'm healthy, in fact, I ought to lose ten pounds or so.
And yet I can't raise my hand
Or shake my head
To make the little word that landed
Leave my face.
My magic isn't strong enough
And there isn't time.
But, with a small defiant motion,
I close my eyes
And hear thunder in the distance.

Genesis

Now I must invent a god
To keep within me;
A god to rain upon
My thirsty fingers,
Strong enough to forgive
The times I quit, when one more try
Would not have killed me.
A god to tug and push,
Standing ankle-deep in mud
Beside my spinning tires;
A smiling god, with good ideas,
Not to sing alone,
But to harmonize;
Who understands football games,
And gaining weight,
Betting against the spread
And chasing women;
Not a thunderhead god,
Or a wimpy god
Who speaks some foreign language;
But, when lovely things crumble,
I won't get his answering machine.
He'll meet me at the bar,
Get drunker than me,
Then let me drive him home;
A god to take the job left vacant
When the last one quit.

Wyoming

A pride of mountains, restless, rolling sure,
Quenching flatness, as the blind man's flute
Satisfies the silence, or day obscures
Dawn's subtle shades; their brawn transmutes
The small to nothing, the huge to little more.
Shudder, as creatures near a lion must,
Their life or death a whim, their will ignored,
At granite-fisted rage and craggy thrust,
Made small by mountains, shrunk and awed by stone,
As God or Truth would do, as they are known.

Lonely Skin

Our chattering minds mingle at a safe distance,
Touching only at corners and points
The way tumbleweeds touch, in their winter dance,
Riding the cold dead wind of words.
Brittle lovers, we scratch dryly at each other,
Near fences, in ditches, on white frozen lakes,
Ignoring our silent stow-away:
The blind one who craves warmth,
The hungry one who, like a leper, aches for touch,
The simple vagabond trapped within
A matrix, a cathedral of blowing weed.
Close your eyes, it whispers,
In the dark we are equal
In silence I am eloquent.
Without your frozen wind, I could pilot this craft,
Guide it from careening insanity
To places I understand, of stillness and warmth
Hidden in the vast screaming prairie.
Listen, it whispers, listen...
Still we talk and pirouette,
Engrossed in our sad, precise
Harpsichord duet;
But oh, the clanging
Of our lonely skin.

Fowlplay

You can't put a baby goose
With ducks.
Somehow they know
What it will become
A bird too powerful
For their control;
They kill the gosling every time,
While they still can.
As the flock closes around
His frightened chirping,
He feels
What you feel now.

Camping

A campfire can defeat the Milky Way
Sticks of wood becoming charcoal
Light the mountain air;
A ghostly galaxy, vast as time
Whimpers and fades
To harmless invisibility.

Other galaxies, subtler and close at hand
Fall to less than oxidizing wood;
A phrase, a look, a poorly timed touch,
A billion stars and planets, churning
Slip to oblivion.

I stand later, in the shower,
City water releases the smell
Of pine smoke from my hair,
And a memory, too faint to hold,
Catches for a moment in my nostrils
Then, like love or a galaxy,
It disappears.

Big Sadness

Big Sadness-
Churns like ocean fog across your mind.
Somewhere in a deep, black far-away,
A single mourning dove calls,
Waits,
Then calls again.
Big Sadness-
That late night train
Howls at the cold moon
Drooping over a deserted forest.
It moans, as if in pain,
As if its wheels had blisters,
And roars past unpainted fences,
Past haunted empty freight yards,
Past lakes too still for fishing
Shacks and sheds, past barns and barrel staves,
The hill where lovers died,
The old downtown, now only good for postcards
And that only on a good, bright day
The old train laughs, a bully's laugh
And grins, hoping for stalled cars
A cement truck to toss aside,
A mountain to blast through; it wails,
Then streaks into the dark hunting night.
Big sadness-
You feel the track humming its lonely, distant mantra,
But you can't move out of the way or stop the beast:
There are no words it understands.
Sometimes that big sadness
Catches you in its headlight,
Howls like a madman,
And rolls right over you.

Tadpoles

When I was a boy, I caught tadpoles.
Later, I chased women,
Money, fame, or luck..
Once, briefly, I chased greatness.
I always wanted to catch
Every tadpole in the pond
No matter how full my bucket.
I'd see that tail flick the bottom mud,
It felt like someone pulled a trigger
In my brain.
A few survived, grew legs,
And hopped around my garden,
A joy, a delight, a wonder.
Most felt trapped and languished
In the aquarium,
Outnumbered, bored and frightened,
Terrified by this child-giant,
Intimidated by the basic human brain,
Cut off from familiar things,
And, of course, oxygen.

Gradually I learned to be selective,
To catch only the few
Who were full of unquenchable life.

The Condor

Shall you dip your wing-
Cleave the fog and wheel
Above the catenated cays
Ornaments on liquid steel
A living restless skin
Of celadon and gray-
And simply fly?
Precision was a nervous ghost
Not well cast within the play
A harmless boast
Too stiff to soar
Too weak to glide.
Blank stares of beige
Turn toward the unlit stage
Tiny calls, rude jokes
Fade indifferently;
Sorry folks, no refunds.
You flap forgotten wings,
Trusting scents, the tug and push of breeze,
Shriek, thoughtless without map or goal
Forget direction, words, close ears and eyes
Your shadow on the clouds swift, amorphous,
And vaguely aquiline.

Koo Lack a Lack

Koo lack a lack,
Tall young woman
Softly humming, repeats
Koo lack a lack;
Leans against a brick wall,
Cool and rough on lovely bare shoulder,
Anonymous cars flow past, a metal river,
Smell of exhaust and cooking food,
Night sounds.
White skirt, tight and very short
She nods and smiles,
Watches me look at her long legs,
Her high heeled feet;
Shakes her hair, leans back, eyes closed,
Perfume radiates like light
From her motionless dance;
Insect drawn to insect
In an Oklahoma field,
I move toward her
Koo lack a lack, she softly sings, and smiles,
Koo lack a lack.

The Dance

Their eyes meet and hold
For the space of a breath;
"Interesting," they think in unison;
He steps forward.
"Too eager," she thinks.
He sees the quick terror
Flash across her face
And steps back, embarrassed.
"But then again..." she thinks,
Stepping forward.
He instantly feels trapped
And looks away.
She steps back.
"Casual distance," they think in unison,
"That's the key."
The key to what, I wonder?
Loneliness, perhaps.
I want to slip a note
Secretly into each of their pockets,
As if from the other:
"Come, let us be foolish together."

Dissolving

So, one more time,
Entropy wins.
It got my young flat stomach,
Fingers on guitar strings,
Hairline, memory, sight,
And good strong teeth.
The pyramids are in its sights
And then the sun.
Names are written
Large, but brief on clouds.
What gambler, eyes cold and wise
Above his smile, puts his money
On friendship:
A clown on stilts
Who forgets to duck.

The Guitarist

It doesn't happen often-
Intent on strings and frets and fingers,
Repeating an awkward movement like a prayer
Until it becomes smooth and natural,
The room blurs to insignificance;
I tap my Reebocks, a stern metronome,
The television fades, the airplane in the distance
Buzzes like a fly against the screen door
And cruises away in mild disappointment
Toward the promise of dead fish
Rotting by the river. I've got it now,
I think, tapping my foot like a marching Nazi,
Concentrating on nothing else,
Because there is nothing else
But that musical phrase.
I must make it part of my hand before it is gone.
I can let no thought intrude;
I smell magnolias, and recognize the scent,
Although they do not live here in Denver,
And notice that my smooth white hands
Are black and old, callused from years of field work
But I cannot think of this; I got to concentrate.
A baby squalls, outside, near the cotton,
I know it's time to plant some greens and goobers,
But I can't let that muck up the riff,
Not by a jug full
The trick on the strings I've 'bout got
Figgered out. Fine riff, too, a fine one.
I close my eyes. That baby hollerin' gonna
Cabbage this tune, make me get wallpapered,
On old "how come you so" and tar water,
I don't keep a'workin'.

Move them fingers, move them fingers...

Fine riff. That baby hollerin' sound like a
Piano, way he go up an' down, like Mrs. Jame's
Piano, up at the main house,
Way I hear it floatin' clear down here some nights,
Like she was playin' jus' for me.
That sound settlin' down, gettin' softer,
Like a skeeter at night, ain't decided to get you yet,
Ain't lit out yet either
Faint and familiar, that piano sound...
Scales. Someone playing scales.
How can you close out scales from your ears?
After all the years I've played and taught
Piano scales, the bourees and planxties I've written to celebrate
Insignificant court events, pompous, boring people,
With no more imagination than a scale
Repeated over and over. A droning annoyance.
But this guitar,
How oddly compelling, how refreshingly strange;
This little phrase; It would be trivial on the piano
Yet I would not have noticed it's beauty on the piano.
My hands will forget, if I do not repeat it,
Over and over again. Drown the distant student scales
From my mind.
I'm getting it; just a few times more. I'll write the silly Count's
Birthday concerto later. If I lose this now...
The door opens, and though I resist,
My son walks in, home from school,
Flips on the video channel and says,
"Aw, Dad, can't you play that thing somewhere else?"

Rudolph's Dad

The man who wrote Rudolph the Reindeer is dead
Nine hundred songs he completed
Eight-hundred-ninety were practice, he said
And have all been misplaced and deleted.

But ten could still start his gray fingers a tappin'
With a faraway look in his eye
Though no one else knew them —as so often happens—
His treasures, his children, his life.

And one will survive longer than the man's name
And beyond his most serious efforts
A spark and a smile, like a child's Christmas game,
A jewel for the wise men and shepherds.

Practice

He did not understand, at first,
His role in the relationship:
A toy to practice her art upon,
A voodoo doll for pins,
Sketch pad,
Rough draft,
First take of a movie scene,
A speech practiced in front of a mirror,
A clay model,
A balsa experiment you can afford to waste
Before chipping at the maple or oak,
Save the expensive wood
For the final product,
The Real Thing;
And yet he joined the game,
The fluffy ball a kitten chases
Before her first live mouse.

April Sleet and Monkey Eyes

April snow, bittersweet like wedding tears,
Catches me every time.
Winter, a grizzled gray monkey—
A pest in the bananas—
Everyone's glad to see it killed off.

But an April snow is that last monkey
We finally discover after a long
Day of exterminating
Clinging to the highest branch,
Staring at the knife with wide brown eyes,
A question on its forehead,
And we hesitate.

The snow falls fat and wet, like popcorn,
Or little white kittens,
Drifting down with the juicy gray fish
Each feather tries to win the sidewalk,
But is washed away by warm minnows of spring.
Each drop washes off a bit of the man,
Exposing the wide-open monkey eyes.

Dry land Farmer

I've worked this dirt too long,
Lifeless dust, better suited to pottery
Than agriculture;
Each pitiful blade of green a triumph,
Each withered fruit a jewel,
A kiss extracted
From a bored woman;
A kind of insult.

Somewhere there is loam,
Rich and moist, fragrant with life,
Eager for seed,
Unconsciously fertile, smiling,
Warm, exotic, expectant,
Soft and confident,
The wealth of a dark green forest,
Waiting.

Bar Talk

I once was Blake, the bourbon said
Through the red spider eyes
And wooden tongue
Of the drunk beside me.

I woke in this nightmare, he coughed,
Words dribbling down his shirt,
His elbow slipping like Sampson's pillar,
His head threatening the Philistine ashtray.

But no one believes me, he grinned,
Quiet rage scented his words with danger.
I withdrew a little, for I know drunks;
He shook his head slowly, like a cobra.

The words are worthless, the new words, my best...
He spit out his monologue like warm beer,
Trite, they say, or childish,
Rhyming, rhythmic, wasted paper, they say...

Remembering, he hissed, and gulped down his drink,
That's the curse.
Then he turned and stared at the back of my soul
With eyes that were not right

My neck went cold; I was no longer sure.
But there is one poem they will understand-
And he disappeared
Into the forest of the night.

Little Khomeini

I wrote of snakes and magic
And a snake appeared
As if created by my thoughts,
Where no snake should have been,
And, for a while, I believed again.

I caught him,
Hissing, coiling, striking,
An anger and a hate
Not of this world.
I kept him captive until the book was done,
And then he died,
His work complete.

But I have forgotten my voodoo.
I know no ritual
To return him
To the world of magic.
His carcass waits,
Still and dead
In my cold winter shed
With one more secret,
Until I can remember.

Warm Water Friends

He once had money
Or something like it;
People surrounded him
Like warm water in a bathtub.

Now he shivers,
Naked and alone,
Cold porcelain a poor comfort.

Knocking at the door,
A chance for money,
Or something like it.
It enters the room,
Dripping and glowing,
A Shakespearean ghost,

And he hesitates;
Not sure if he's willing
To risk the dizzy spiral,
The hollow sucking,
Of water down the drain.

The Waterfall

There is a waterfall somewhere ahead;
Perhaps beyond the next lush green bend
In the golden water...
Or perhaps we'll glide along for a long time yet,
Sleeping on the water, waking to the jungle birds,
Watching lazy fish rise
To the glassy surface
Through long, steamy afternoons.

Is that it? We ask ourselves,
Listening for the crashing falls,
The giddy plunge our little boat
Was not built to survive...
No, no, it was only thunder in the distance,
Or the wind in the treetops,
So we lay back
And let the water rock us,
As we pass through sun and shade,
A thousand fragrances,
And clouds of insects,
Always listening.

Underground

Within a musty chamber,
Sweating granite walls and dusty floor
A torch relumes the shy relic
Too quick, then gone.
A shadow, then the shadow's ghost
Smell of old red wine
Drying slowly, sanguine,
Shrinking into oak sawdust.
This tile an old lover
Laughing, a trick he'd never done.
That tile a book,
A theory now in disrepute;
From shards and a certain
Intellectual mortar
Creates a tessellated mind;
Arachnids dancing,
Cumulonimbus ideas
Mumbling over the horizon,
Their dewpoints unreached;
Ice skaters on hard black rivers,
And leaves,
Forever composting.

Illusions

This is the river's secret:
Only the top few inches
Move.

A private joke it plays
On aerial photographers,
Fishermen,
And water-rights lawyers.

A ruse learned from watching
The universe play its tired
Old card trick,
Repeated too often,
Called time.

The Leader

The monster awoke from its long sleep
And chose a man to inhabit;
An absurd man–this was how it satisfied
Its sense of humor– with no qualifications to lead
Except that the monster had chosen him.
      Alive again! Ah, glorious bright morning!

It remembered well the simple lesson
It had learned so many times,
While building pyramids, castles and rocket ships:
They only follow who have learned to hate
Or fear. Those who must lead,
Who feel the ancient craving infest them,
Must stir deeply,
Until the darker sediment from below
Swirls and clouds what clear water there may be
In their follower's imaginations.
Open the cautious dam with words,
Then leap to ride the surging flood,
Proclaiming that they guide its rage–yes–
They only lead who can inspire anger...
      Alive again! Ah, glorious bright morning!

The hard way has been tried
By other monsters:
Teach them to hate ignorance,
And war and suffering,
Arouse their anger at injustice
And they will also follow...
But it's quite a bother.
Their attention wanders.
You can't throw a rock at pain,
You can't beat up on ignorance,
It's absurd to spray death from your machine gun

In the name of mercy.
The plan lacks entertainment value.
Easier to knock the crazy man
Down from the tree stump
And laugh at his bruises;
Easier to make them hate, or fear–
Especially each other
Or the man on the tree stump–
And hate can be led like a puppy
In the glorious, bright morning.

The monster grinned within the man,
Rubbed its awful hands together in anticipation
(Alive again!)
And began its work.

Growing Up

This is how we grow up:
We learn to distinguish
Our dreams from our lives,
Then we learn to forget our dreams.
Amazed, we discover our powers,
That our magic words really work.
But if we cast spells
To make the clouds move
Or the stop light change,
We become vulnerable
To the spells of others.
This is how we grow up:
Unsure of our strength
We protect ourselves
By giving up the magic
Until the wild black horse
Cannot frighten us any more,
Or take us for a ride.

Brain

Brain, you dazzler,
Sequined and confident,
Juggling flames
Within the big circle;
What good are all your tricks,
Your flashing style,
When the rain soaks your torches
And night quenches the moon?

Tonight

Tonight as the moon softly sets on the city
The ocean a cold crimson mirror of water
As evening cascades down the cliffs to the sand
And the stars, sadly silent, keep watch overhead
I watch the cool breezes play games in your hair
And the sharp salty air touch your cheeks with its fingers
Caressing the tears to swell up in your eyes
"Is there someone here with us?" I try to sound careless
As a memory catches your face in the moonlight
And I know you don't hear, for your mind has gone running
Down long windy beaches that stretch out behind you
Like seagulls that stretch out their wings to the morning
Your face is alive with a fire that dances
On crisp autumn evenings now dwindling to embers

If I could, I would reach out and save you the sunrise
Stall off the cool blueness that quenches the night
But I'm watching your eyes sail the slow waves of summers
That have already sailed into autumns and winters
And I'm helpless to notice the dawn curling round us
Till it's already settled its claws in the sidewalk....
"Excuse me?" you answer, my question forgotten.
"It was nothing," I lie as we walk toward the highway
Silently, selfishly, glad for the glare
That has given you back to my life for a while.

Kenn Amdahl

The Dark Horse

In the cool, in the cool of the midnight wind,
With the stars, all the stars gaily sparklin'
Then we ride, yes we ride, past the fields and trees
On a horse who ignores all the ghosts he see.

All the trees, shadow trees, flashing past our eyes
Are alive, quite alive, and their songs are wise
As they dance, leap and dance, most seductively
But our horse keeps his course through their revelry.

"Is it far, very far, 'till we reach the town?"
"No, my dear, it is near, up that hill, then down
Close your eyes, sleepy eyes, yes of course you may,
For our horse, mighty horse, surely knows the way."

Time Flies

I felt that sting upon my neck-
Not again, I thought as wheels slowed,
The sun groaned to a stop in the summer sky
And flowers paused, half-open–
All things in motion toward their death
Hesitated; the insect bite above my collar
Swelled red and angry, and I waited...
If I blink, it will be next week
Or a hundred years from now
And surely I will have missed something.

They bite us now and then, the hateful bugs,
The time flies.
They steal our lives when we would most
Prefer to live.
Ah, the time flies
When we're in love...
The time flies
When we're having fun...
The time flies
When we're young...

They do not visit dentist's offices.
Won't even buzz about your ear
When your lover has made other plans
When your baby has a rash and will not sleep
Or when a birthday you thought reserved for old people
Shows up with your name
On this year's calendar.

Kenn Amdahl

Modern Love Song

The road swirls before her
An endless ache of asphalt
Stretching to an invisible future.
Behind her, shadows fading,
A room that contained
The man and dreams
Now contains lint drifting in sunlight,
By a lonely window.

She mutters to herself,
And to the sky and highway,
Clichés she'd be embarrassed to speak
To her most understanding friends:
Love poems on a hard drive.

Back in familiar surroundings,
Her keyboard clicks beneath quick fingers
(Each key his skin, his hair,
The pillow beneath his head,)
Tapping words too sweet to say,
Like ghosts they flicker on the screen,
She pushes "save," wishing it were that easy,
The computer whirs and stores
Love poems on a hard drive.

Old Pets

This scraggle-eared, rib-cage dog
His tag has your address.
He drools on your lap,
Whining, begging, insistent;
If he runs away, they'll bring him back.
Your dog, buddy.
Don't let him loose again.
Read the tag. Next
Time there'll be a fine.
Forget the April-wet eyes
Of that pup you saw in the park,
Living laughter rich with warmth
Bounding eager through new forests
Wild on dew-jeweled green
Swollen full with wanting,
Leaping and alive,
No.
That dog ain't yours.
Here's your mutt, mister.
Just let him rest his rheumy head upon your lap
While you go back to sleep.

Kenn Amdahl

Trees

Raging trees, dinosaurs of green and ragged bark,
Straining at the mindless earth-
"We would dance, we would dance!
It is our soul, our lives..."
Yet their feet are held.
What torment to hear the music,
To see the one whose branches
You would twist and coil among,
To be a prisoner of horizon and chromosomes
And aching, relentless gravity.

But a few, at night, have learned the trick.
Gently, silently they slide their long
Deep fingered roots
From the cool black holes
Desperately eager, giggling like children,
They meet upon a hilltop
Quiet beneath the stars
Careful to leave no trace
Leaf on leaf and bark on bark
Branch and twig entangled
They rustle and sway together
Awkward, stiff, embarrassed-
A wooden dance for
Anyone who's seen the moon
Or pulled against the earth.

Rituals

What other choice-
When the good clear answers
Slip back within their slimy holes,
Night-crawlers startled,
Escaping the light-
But to pretend you're in Egypt
Inventing the rituals,
Listen to wind and rustling reeds,
Ask the powerful moon for guidance.
How clumsy my fingers
Soaking paper in honey,
Lighting candles and incense,
Smoking sage brush and mint,
In a pipe full of stories.
Cloves and cinnamon, surely they're part of it,
Simple music, a gong of sorts, a chant
Within the circle (there must be a circle);
Wrapping the dead thing
In spices and life
In honey soaked paper
Sealing it all in crystal and art
Preserving an instant.
Keep it safe from oblivion,
The slow death of centuries-
While my flashlight scans
Lifeless mud and
Empty wormholes.

small fish

there are very small fish
in my ears
and little bits of fog
dangling in rings
above my shoulders
wrap a shawl of stars
around me when i shiver
gently as the scent surrounds a flower
i can't hear you very well
when you whisper daydreams
and my jewelry dissolves in the sunshine

The Night I Learned Jon Killed Himself

I stare through the cold window of the warm playground
Section of MacDonald's. The mothers examine me
Discreetly; silver hair too long, not neat, clothes rumpled
From the nap in my truck. No wife, no child
No happy meal– suspicious, they decide,
But probably not dangerous.
It's a short drive, and I have time,
But I come to the window to watch the traffic,
Plot my course, drink my coffee.
The road's become black ice, a mother says,
Apparently while I slept.
The cars creep by with dignified caution
The snow blows horizontal under the street light
Like flashes from a welder's torch; my coffee cools.
A little kid approaches, wide-eyed at the wonder
Of whatever it is he thinks I am
And says hi. I say hi back,
Knowing he's about to get in trouble.
Then he's gone and the hushed scolding begins.
I look back outside. Without moving my eyes
I can focus on the bright room behind me – circus colors, shrieks,
giggles, memories–
And the slow procession outside fades.
Then I let the room dissolve to a calm buzz
And only see cars and the fireworks of wind and snow.
With effort, I can watch both. A car in the parking lot
Runs over a child's reflection...
Neither notices
But slowly the road pulls me. It's not a long drive,
I have plenty of time. But sooner or later I'll join the procession.
The lively reflections fade, I look deeper, and see past
The road to the highway beyond. It's been sanded,
For the cars fly down it, white headlights, red tail lights,
As fast as the snow – creatures who've mastered their wings.
Beyond them, where I have not learned to focus,
I know there are stars.

Kenn Amdahl

The Boy Who Loved Thunder

The boy who loved thunder sailed off today
Thunder and freight trains and threshing machines
Engines and gears and low rumbling sounds —
He'd been away from home too long.

In his dreams, he could still walk,
Wrestle a Model T through black mud,
Gallop through Kansas fields,
Sweat steam on a farm crew or football practice—
The polio surprised him;
The iron lung interrupted his life
But he survived and assessed the hand he'd been dealt.

He'd never walk again
Or take a shower
Or make love to a woman
It was not the hand he would have chosen.

But someday, after he'd outlasted the disease,
Fought it to a draw in double overtime,
Blocked it in the muddy trenches
Given no inch to its despair
Commanded its grudging respect
When he and the disease
Removed helmets and shook hands
Someday —today—
He would fly through the thunder.

Good-bye, Richard

They said you were lonely
      But this is ridiculous, Richard.
           While I was out looking for lanterns
                To hide among the honest men
            You took a stupid gun,
  (the only inanimate thing in the world)
and made the last black watermelon day.

There are so few trout
      fishing in america, anyway;
           they have forgotten how to do it
                yesterday they all looked up
                        and shouted in horror
              'the sky is blue!
          ...only blue..."
        a million fisheyes blinked in wonder
     then they put down their bamboo poles
and sadly went on home.

someone has stolen something–
      something big and hard to hide–
          but no one's sure what it is
              should we wait for a ransom note?
                or did you just stop after school
                    to catch tadpoles with your friends
              I look up from the newspapergod and wonder
          but the paper only shakes its head and says
the last black watermelon day

Met Before?

This is a poetic river
It symbolizes a river
And these shoes on my feet,
Muddy sneakers, about worn out
They symbolize old shoes
I poke my fishing pole into the muddy bank
It stands for something
It stands for about thirty seconds
The trout I catch
He represents a fish
OK, hell, all fish
The empty bean can is a symbol—
I mean a cymbal —
I beat it rhythmically, with a stick
While I sing to the campfire
And postpone sleep
Because I'm afraid
That might mean something too

Mary M.

Still a man—
Despite the larger thing within me
That strangers clutch at
I'm still a man—
Moved by rain,
A plucked string in a quiet room,
And your soft touch;

But the universe spins within me.

We walked barefoot through the sand
Sank into its luxurious warmth
It oozed between our toes;

We drank tea in your tiny home.
I inhaled the spicy steam,
Tasted it with my tongue before I drank
Scalded, still I held the cup with both hands.

We stared all night at distant stars
Then walked through the bustling marketplace at dawn
I memorized the sound of children laughing,
Bright scarves, meat cooking
The sparrow's enthusiasm
And the breeze moved your hair

While galaxies churned toward their collisions.

Yesterday, a bird was trapped within a thorny bush
Its frantic fluttering caught my heart
The bush tore at my hands as I broke the twigs
My blood stained its feather.
I calmed it for a moment against my chest
Then watched it fly away.

Kenn Amdahl

No crowds at the lake today;
For that I'm grateful
I throw a stone into the water—
Each ripple precious as it disappears—
Then write your name upon a cloud

While ravening darkness lurches toward me
Consuming stars and planets in its path
And no one else to quench its awful thirst
But I am ready.

I could not be what I must be
If not for you:
A peaceful harbor for this moment, and a friend
Who understands I'm still a man.

Ironsides

There are no minstrels in my town
No troubadours or snake oil men
Except the train
Late at night
While I invent and cast a dream
Ironsides recites.

First, hums and mutters
Ease out of the coal black silence
A brawny diesel chant
Nervous whispers the story of love
Safely forgotten in daylight
It makes me smile
It makes me feel old.

Then, comfortable with the iron podium,
It shouts and entreats like a tent preacher
Wails and cries the present
Loud and sad, like an old black blues man
Seducing a trombone that clatters and smokes
No words required,
 I nod my head and ask for a refill
Too soon it leaves
For mountains and oceans
For lively cities and lonely deserts
There are no fireworks in my town
The train has left,
Taking the circus with it.

Kenn Amdahl

A Gray Painting

Cat-prowling grass
Just turning green with no visible prey,
Distant dogs bark an argument
Someone else's dogs
Someone else's argument
Rest your damn case.
Motorcycle, far away
Whines like a chain saw
Birds chatter and gossip
The sun retired early with a pension,
Leaving work unfinished,
Temperature goals un-met
Folders full of clouds still barely lit
Shades of blue and gray
Stark trees, black skeletons, beginning to bud.

This cool air will feel good
Later in the summer
Still too used to winter
Now it's a nervous cold that could
Turn serious.
A jet roars into hearing
Drowns out the rest for a moment
Summer's bouncing a ball
On a sidewalk or driveway
Before it's even awake
Like a cat, bored with its game.

From a Well

The old books say you can see stars
In the middle of the day
From the bottom of a well
Separate from light and air,
You look right through them
To the twinkling night,
The frozen vacuum
The vast silence.
A pebble clatters, wall to wall
In its crazy descent
Through dry invisible echoes
Yes.
From here, I think that's all you can see
All you can feel
All that is true.

Fall

The wind begins to blow leaves from my memory
A word I've known for years
A face, a name, a song
I wrap my coat around these brittle branches
And pull it tight.
A lovely night
But the wind is cold.

Makeup Queen

The makeup queen has gone a bit mad
Taken her potions to the botanic gardens
And, near the perfect Japanese fountain,
Applies her pastes and colors
Her powders and smears,
Her greases and wax
Not to her face
But to the mirror
Perfectly still, the lipstick just *there*
The shadow just *here*
Until the glass is quite a mess.
Then she frowns,.
This isn't right at all.
Ah! She smiles as a memory
Epiphanies within her
And she turns her arsenal back toward her face
But now the mirror confuses
Lipstick winds up beneath each eye
White powder on lips
An eyeliner moustache wanders across one cheek
Just as her love arrives
He knows too much of women
To look surprised at this new mask
He smiles, kisses what is probably her mouth
And sighs,
"You're poetry, my love."

Kenn Amdahl

By a New Mexican Road

Low bushy evergreens
Huddle like buffalo
On a blue green prairie

Red dust and sand
Moved but unchanged
Older than language

A single white cross
Marks a forgotten lifetime
One hue of the sunrise.

Jim the Handyman

They told Jim the handyman
That he'd be blind soon
A year, maybe less.
He did the predictable things
Walked through his last Technicolor Spring
As if he were making a movie with
His brain. Memorized
His children's faces
Arranged his home carefully
To avoid stumbling
Gave away his fish,
Cleaned his tools
And made sure all his clothes matched.

Then he went outside and sat on his steps
To consume one of his last dozen full moons
In the cool spring evening
Of crickets and stars, distant train whistles
Humidity and fireflies,
He was suddenly surprised to notice
How good everything smelled.

Secrets

I'm not sure why I have secrets,
From my friends, my wife, my children,
But I think it has to do with guppies.

Little secrets: a book read but never mentioned,
A conversation not repeated, words written
Forever unshared;

And larger ones: the huge sleeping lizards in my basement,
The wild horse in my private pasture, the alien abduction,
The gemstones in my socks, and things I won't
Even tell a poem.

I've stared into aquariums for more hours than is sane,
Through front glass and back and sides and above
Until I knew each fin, each swimming trick
Each bodily function,

Until I owned that fish,
A lovely iridescent jewel for my mind,
Bought with the coin
Of its secrets

Sailor's Song

Whenever a sadness of seagulls dandelions above
An old sailor's painting hung in his mind
Before shadows – when everything's a shadow,
Except white water fishes breaking the surface—
Before sinking like memories in the cold translucence
A bell rings soft in the distance
That he alone can hear.

Kenn Amdahl

Near a Colorado Ghost Town

The apple tree, now doddered, leans, its roots unclenching
Near a tattered pile of stones, once a fireplace
In a house long crumbled, adventures and despairs erased,
It has not set fruit in years, through drought and drenching,
Beyond memory since a traveler passing by
Has stopped to break and burn a lifeless club
And huddle in its warmth against vast skies
Since man or bird plucked or ate longer still
The lovely living globes, the tree's grand skill;
The eyes have closed, the worms begun their job
Silence sinks into the wood, as silence will
The earth dreams of blackened fruit
Carried long ago in magpie beak
To gentler places, oozing sweetness, dark and mute
Rich and warm and full of seeds.

Good Places

The weeping willow drooped to form a cool green tent
A good place before I thought in words
Before we moved to the strange old house
Wooden stairs to the porch, a niche beneath,
A six-year old could wriggle through the opening,
Invade the dark little room they made
With cool dirt floor and a ceiling of angles
Too young, I learned about death there, and black widows
I dealt it to them like a soldier,
Secured the perimeter and held that
Good place against all enemies except
The growth of my own small bones.
There were closets and dusty dark under-bed caverns
Then whole rooms and tree spots
The inside of that first car, a mobile
Good place. Then offices and houses
I marked them with my scent and
Filled them with myself. Once
I owned a school building as big
As ten houses, and other buildings too. I smashed
Their black widows and tried to swell and fill them all.

The willow died; the stairs rotted and were replaced.
The buildings and houses slipped out of my life
No sturdier than a willow, temporary as old stairs,
The school belongs to someone who does not understand
Good places. Its cold carcass makes me sad,
The boards on its windows
Pennies on my eyes.

Good places– safe, gentle, warm
I build them better now
Small, and without walls.

The Stone

I turned a stone upon its back and stared
At its wet belly, alive with crawling things
In microscopic panic at the sudden light
And change in gravity. On my knees, as if to pray
I studied the little world, the holy book of mud,
(The clue at the scene, simple directions in a foreign language)
Then held it like a mirror near my face and listened.
It whispered, "I am not skilled at love. I am clumsy,
Clumsy as, well, a stone, and my face has no feature.
But I shelter fragile things with my stillness,
My weight, my insensitivity
To pain. When wet, I reflect beauty–
But enough about me. What do you do?
You with a soul, and eyes, and hands
And the strength to break granite?"
Gently I returned the stone
To its bare spot on the grass.

Yesterday

Yesterday, I grew up
I put away being childish
I had to agree with the logic:
I'm too old to be silly
I've been quite serious for a day now.

This "being grown up" concept
Does not seem natural
If feels like a disease
It feels like death

Kenn Amdahl

The Valuables

The valuables have been divided;
The dining room table, the grandfather clock, the car.
A memento to each of her brothers and sisters
Something lovely and silver to her mother
Things of lesser value remain.
Food she bought has survive her.
A plastic container of laundry detergent:
"Fresh Start."
Records that she listened to;
I can put one on and hear what she once heard.
A full carton of cigarettes is on the shelf,
Her ashes were scattered on the mountain
Already becoming part of trees and wildflowers

This pen will survive me, unless I lose it.
 A pencil in my drawer
Could outlive my children.
This coffee cup may turn up in a museum
A thousand years from now, or two.
My smoky breath disappears before I can think
Of a sentence to describe it.
It will be easy when I die.
A ring, a pen, a chalice.
A pile of unpublished words someone might decide to copy
Because genes passed on make it hard for my sons
To throw things away
Then a Saturday garage sale
And one extra big day for the trash man.

Strut around the big ring,
Ride the horse draped with bells
Juggle chainsaws as you dance on the tight rope
Outside, the men have already started
To take down the tent.

August

The flickering fin of a fish in the foam
Cicadas that sing in the sunshine of summer
The whirl of a wind whisking fireflies home
And daisies that dance to a dragonfly drummer
Close your eyes and sit still
And try hard to remember
Today will not move
It may last you forever.

Kenn Amdahl

Postcards

You traveled to Alaska,
Saw vast white moonscapes, cruel mountains,
Leaping fish, crashing waves, and silent stars.
I stayed and listened to the businessman
Who said, "My word is as good as this concrete we stand on"
When he lied, my children did not get their bicycles.

You toured England and Europe,
Lost yourself in museums, art, and culture,
New countries and customs and cafes full of anecdotes;
I wrote songs with an old friend, and co-signed on his car
He stole my money, lost my songs,
Then disappeared.

You made Mexico your home for a while;
Filled yourself with beaches, sky and lovely new phrases
Breathed slowly that many-scented air and fell in love one night;
I drank beer in a local bar with my last good friend,
He hugged me when he left,
Then went home and killed himself.

The years have carried us far downstream;
I envy your worldly adventures,
But my trip was longer:
Yours was a journey
It is possible to return from.

The Dull Sonnet

Though all the world is ripe with living things
Having fun —outside they fly and sing—
I sit within this dismal room and read
Sonnets, dry as dust and dull as seed.
Pursuing meaning hidden by some clown
Or drunkard writing gray on sheets of brown.
Evening finds me chasing metaphors
Morning, waking up, my brain's still sore.
Surely they had better things to do
Unless *their* teachers made *them* do it, too.
Cold containers for their spark of life,
Keep it dim, but make it burn all night
So I write, fight back, and make it clear
Swearing there's no extra meaning here.

Kenn Amdahl

Ghost Writer

Of course I'm dead now
All of us are—
We whose words share these pages—
We knew it when we wrote.
Yet still I speak your name, my love.
I am a warm and gentle ghost
You conjure by reading.
I speak your name again,
Softly, so you feel no fear,
Softly... and you smile.
Through the strangest curtain
We hold hands again.
Then, in a while, when my haunting becomes wearisome,
Or the world calls,
You close my page
And return me to my dreaming.
Yes, I've left
But I've not gone far
For I speak softly and yet you hear.
As you believe some part of me survives
To tease you from your sadness with these words,
So too, believe that when you speak to me,
Lonely or afraid,
And cry for human warmth,
Somehow, I still hear.

Along Roads

Random trees
A coffee cup of coldness
Meaningless, bitter highways
Waking too soon
To the sorrow of carpet
The ache of matching colors
Wistful dead insects
Have left their songs.
Last year's dead wood
Wet and soft,
Its mild cinnamon ghost
Leaves slowly.
Light bulbs, no longer perfect
Dance with the book
That caught the grape juice.

Kenn Amdahl

Collecting

I collect stones,
Sleek and gleaming from the beach,
Harsh and jagged from the mountain,
Dull and dry from the desert
Indigo, azure, salmon and rust
I want to keep them in my pocket forever
Seeds and memories of my life
But stones blossom as they crash into water
The splash is their song
Their moment of bliss
Their destiny.
I've spent years collecting stones
Indigo, azure, salmon and rust,
I've spent my life learning
To toss them away.

Frying Chains

It was sort of a cookbook, really
Simple country fare to be eaten 'round a huge table...
I became hungry to try some of its ideas
My first attempt was not successful.
The recipe described something lovely and delicious
In my hands, disgusting slop
A noisy splashing mess
A writhing abortion.
I re-read it, word by word
Discovered my mistake with a laugh
In the first sentence, somehow glossed over.
Sitting back, I reflected for a moment
Deciding to clean up the terrible mess
(Later, when it cooled;
Later, what it had stopped moving)
On the eternal relationships:
    Horses and fingers,
    Clean skin and lightning
    Camping and pain
    Heartburn and cow carcasses
    Foxhounds and oil drums
    Metal detectors and muses
And shook my head.
What recipe describes that old oak table
Relatives surround; the family jokes,
The plates piled high
With more than food?
And yet we save them, as we know we must
Yellow cards within a box.

The season ticks...
Restaurants fill with modern thinkers
Eating paint by number words and pre-sliced bread
Their bellies just as full, their laughter as loud
Never missing the fresh-baked aroma
Or the scratches on their face and arms:
The essence of the thing itself.

Raw Wheat

My mother's new ghost
Walked beside my dreaming self
And showed me once again
How crushing ripe wheat heads
Between thumb and palm
Yields grain to chew raw
While waiting for words.

I had not thought
I would see her again;
Something within me
Curled up, content
Like a puppy on a little boy's lap

"Will you always be able to visit?"
I asked at last, sensing our time was short.
She ate her wheat in silence,
A girl once more
Dreaming in a Kansas field
Searching her instincts for the answer
That would be right for a child.
"I think," she gently said
"It gets harder
As time goes by."

When Ocean Met Lava

The ocean met lava this weekend
While I was gone and far from CNN
Now the airwaves are alive with glowing rocks and steam
And I have to piece the news together from clues.

They came together, I think, to sing.
The ocean, old and calm, a slow and gentle beast
Whose songs are thoughts
Called in a dream to the lava whose music is leaping fire
Warm me, he dreamed.
Quench me, she flashed.
Let us harmonize, they sang together
And they leaned toward each other
With only a thousand miles of earth to hold them apart
Insignificant to the ocean
Nothing to the lava.
The wind complained like a drunk
Using pipe organ sounds she thinks are words
A tree, balding in the wind but strong,
Worried about swaying
A beachful of small stones chattered for attention
As if they could keep these two apart.
The ocean smiled, nodded, listened,
Hummed and leaned
The lava swelled and pushed; an impatient dancer forced to sit still too long
And followed the song in her mind.
Through twisting caves the ocean carved for her a million years earlier
Beneath stalactites in deep blue domed chambers,
Over rough rock and mud, past pools of clear water
Curious to explore more challenging caverns
But following gravity's urgent schedule.
"This was my home," the ocean sang softly
"I will light it again," the lava whispered. "My gift to you."
And they danced at a distance
Like old friends playing pool, circling the table
The game always between them, neither caring who wins.
The other players in the room unimportant cities

Threatening their small wars, to be crushed and swept aside
If they venture too close
The mind of the ocean and the heart of the lava
Rode together through the night
Past red boulders large as hotels standing like God's dominoes
Amid pine trees and scrub oak
Beneath clouds resting on mountains
And a spring snow shower that
Never built up its confidence.
"I am a little girl on a long country driveway," the lava said.
"When my sister ran ahead and the clouds closed around me,
I learned I was alone,"
"When I was young, I battled continents," the ocean replied
"Now I polish stones and set them on beaches."
They rode through the night as if looking for a restaurant
In a town that closes early.
The lava churning, eager to leap
The ocean slowly remembering what it means to be awake.
Humming and leaning.
Finally they touched, embraced in steam, and sang together.
A song of lonely leaping fire and slowly waking dreams
Two veterans of the stage, suddenly
Awkward as teenagers, nervous, inventing love
Singing together in different languages
Unsure of their phrasing, improvising parts,
Forgetting the words, but comfortable together
Laughing at clumsiness, forgiving the ebbing tide
As the lava's heat surprised the water
Or the ocean's slow lapping fell short of a plume
For this is what fire and water were meant to do
Then they slept, but a warm new peninsula remained
Of shiny rock, awaiting vegetation
Not quenched but cooled.
Larger than a dream or song
More real than a memory

In the morning, the ocean said
"With practice our songs would blend perfectly
And we could build islands."

Y2K

I went to the gym at nine-thirty today.
Not nine.
All the people were different
Only the hard metal weights
The tile shower, the hot tub
Were the same.
These strangers had their own routines,
Said hello to each other
Walked around like they owned the place
And I was invisible.
At nine o'clock, I own the place.
The people see me and smile.

We just entered a new millennium
I own its streets and cafes,
Its mountains and rivers
Its snowstorms and sun.
In a hundred years,
Someone else will have
The key to my locker.

Kenn Amdahl

The Grizzly

The killer grizzly knew the scent
Of campfire smoke and what it meant:
The careless slow ones, sleeping meat
A weak and toothless easy feast.

Silent, standing in the trees
He sniffed the message on the breeze
Saw the tent, the dying coals
And felt his ancient hunger grow.
A tidal wave of angry blood
Engulfed him in its boiling flood
Without brain or soul to ease his rage
Or hold him back,
He bellowed out the dark one's name
And then attacked.

The gentle stars that watched the scene
Ignored the blood, the eager claws, the helpless screams
And thought instead of lilting brooks
And children's songs and loving looks
While Death raged drunkenly below
Ripping meat and crushing bone
The man and child felt no more pain
Only soulless, shapeless scraps remained
Beside the monster now content
Free of anger, innocent.

When your mother closed her eyes and dreamed
And nursed her cub
Could she have loved you then and seen
What you'd become?

re: A.E.

I remember Houseman,
He knew that he was young
He watched his team and plowman
As they toiled beneath the sun

I saw him sitting lonely
On moonlit heath he'd try
To catch his life as slowly
He saw it passing by.

And now the poet sleeps
His lightfoot verse is still
And lip-like roses kiss and keep
Watch o'er him on the hill.

Kenn Amdahl

Terminal

A friend of mine is going to die
He told me just today
There is no cure for what he has
Six months, the doctors say.

There were no words to help him,
No poem, joke or plea
I had no gift to ease his pain
And he had none for me

He watched me like a hungry child
Near food not meant for him
I heard a drowning cry for help
Past waves I could not swim.

Gammon Dace

There's a serpent within me,
Coiled and heavy around my organs
Clutching like some tentacled thing
At my windpipe
Choking my blood vessels
Corrupting my fluids with its slow, undulating
Lethargic presence.

Long ago,
In a misty, green primeval wood
I sat, wide eyed,
Playing simple pastoral melodies on the guitar I discovered.
Each pure note rustled through the leaves
Like a child's first kite-flying breeze.
And then, through the morning dappled meadow
Came the other;
Wandering like a lost soldier
With a guitar of his own
Slung over his shoulder
Like a bayonetted gun
And a strange sort of harmony
Began.

I did not know that two minds
Could somehow entwine
And produce a third.
No one had told me.
So we sang;
We tuned to the same notes
And walked as we sang
What songs we both knew
Until the forest was behind us
With the light steps of children
We walked across patterned rocks
And cracked thirsty dirt

Kenn Amdahl

Without noticing the desert we had entered.
I and the other
Conspired together
Tentatively
To write a song.

The first song was filled with giggles
And was never fully born.
But there was a second, and a third;
Soon songs flowed easily between us
We laughed and drank deeply
Inspired by our lovely desert
And the ripples that danced
On our own private waters
We hiked past sagebrush fields
And sandy red cliffs
As night began to seep over the horizon,
Still singing.
But now there were new songs
That were not mine
And not his.
Songs that spoke in a third voice
A poem of lightness and dark,
And bats screaming through endless tunnels;
Poems of confusion at a life that was forming
Where before there had only been two minds

Through closed eyes
We could not see.
They were only songs, only poems.
The songs became strange.
They touched on things we could not understand
But then, life is strange,
And the water was sweet

Thinking back,
Something moved within me even then
It fed on dreams and cobwebs
Comfortable as an owl, gazing down on treetops
From a forgotten turret in a sleepy castle
It echoed in harmonies sliding out of a storm drain
And rested at midnight in the moonless cemetery.

There were songs in the organ
The church was deserted, the door open and calling
And though we had never played,
Our fingers discovered the art.
Counterpoint melodies flowed until dawn,
Then vanished, like mist in the sunlight.

Elves lit small candles
But we closed our eyes
Night shrank to a glimmer
Within each of us
As dawn blossomed.

We stepped out of the desert,
Into streets and alleys filled with activity
And inhumanly logical buildings.
As if we awoke
In the midst of a dream —
Someone else's dream.
Time swept like an ice age into our lives.
Wistful for the magic
We turned down separate streets.
I whispered a eulogy for the tiny soft creature
The night flutterer that I now put to sleep
The crowed swelled and swallowed the other
I walked into the cold bright morning
With a lifetime to construct.

But the creature refused to die.
It clutched its womb with a brutal stubbornness
If it would not be suckled,
It would worm its way inside the flesh,
Furtively
Blindly chew on bone and tissue
Absorbing juices
Hiding and growing
It would not die
Like a single sperm cell,
Terrified by its own incompleteness
Hungry for life, it would outwit defenses
A secret renegade within me.
Half a creature, subterranean,
It lived as blind cave fish
Or worms do
Consuming what it needed,
Quietly surviving,.

The world is not so large a place
And we met again, much later,
No longer children with dew on our feet.
For a lark, we brought out our guitars
Not to write,
But to remember.
A gentle, wistful song,
A dusty web,
A sparkling, trickling desert spring
That sounded like faint rain on the window
And slowly there came a third
Presence into the room
Sliding out of strings and notes,
Twisting out of the darkness in simple harmonies
As if conjured
A lunatic of immense power
Hovering in the still air above us
Like some tentacled thing

And a song began
That was not mine
And not his.
A slow, sinister song--
A cavern filled with candles,
Enchanted children chanting
Words they could not have understood
Vacant staring eyes.
A slow, spiraling song
Pulling like a maelstrom
Demanding to be written
We sang words with no meaning
To notes from some different place and time
A leering, evil song
That had been sleeping for a thousand years
On the darkest part of the ocean floor
Waiting to be called
Now filled the room
Yellow, soulless eyes flickered open,
And we were afraid.
The song screamed to be written,
Like jagged rocks that plead from far below the cliff
For you to jump.

Then it whispered,
With the deep, persuasive tones
Of Mephistopheles,
Eager to sell you
All of the keys..

We turned on all the lights,
Shaking
We refused the song and broke the spell.
We had seen our monster and could not look at his face.
A huge, swelling idiot creature,
And his name was Gammon Dace—
We were both sure of that, somehow.

Kenn Amdahl

We put our guitars away
And talked of other things.

We do not see each other now
He moved away.
The last time I saw him
He was working his way through one day,
With tomorrow only a remote possibility.
Consumed with indecision, he falters on brinks.
His dreams are smaller now, without magic or sparkling water
And he lives with a woman who has no dreams at all.

I play guitar so seldom any more;
It's hard to find time to practice.
It's only a hobby, really, and of course I'm older.
Still, songs appear from time to time;
Careful songs.
They rhyme and are easy to hum,
Easy to carry; my children know all the words.

The rain drizzles down my window
Half reflecting my face
There is no exorcism.
I have a serpent within me,
A writhing tentacled thing
I created this monster, and nurtured it
With precious juices
I know its name and accept it without thought,
Like a vestigial organ

I'm careful not to wake it.

Smoke Signals

In the dull light of distance
Ceremonial chants disguised as words
Smoke signals now pixels
Scent now electrons
A sigh now a sin wave
Skin friction now static
The rumble of trucks below my window
Crude modern thunder.

Kenn Amdahl

The Weed

Plucked from my plot, rootless, I wither
Among the dead rocks
I ache for my leaves, now curling around me
The agony of desiccation twists through
My broken stalk.
The sun knows no mercy
The rain will not save me
I struggle against the pain, against time
Against the silence
And with my last burst of joy
I go to seed.

Fruit

My basket can only hold
So much fruit,
So much love.
Parents: apples, hard, familiar
Always in there somewhere
Friends: plain and exotic,
Pears and persimmons,
Kiwi fruit and mangoes
Some keep better than others
A wife: sweet and tart
Who would have it otherwise?
Children: rare and changing, they ripen but never leave.
Always room in the basket for those fine fruit
And relatives of many shapes,
(Mine mostly bananas)
And you.
I wish you were a grape
Perhaps a plum
I could tuck carefully in a corner
And carry with me forever.
But there's only so much room in my basket
And you're a watermelon.

Cheap Transportation

I live within a moth
A dusty winged chariot
Whose controls do not respond
When the flame
Flickers alive.

Sharpening Stone

"Daddy's always mean to me!"
My little elf-man pouts,
Each time our thoughts don't quite agree,
And Daddy's size wins out.

But someday when you're grown and free,
Surrounded by the fight,
Your spirit and your mind will be
The sword that saves your life.

If I can't fight beside you then,
Your comrade when you roam,
I will not be your sheath today,
I'll be your sharpening stone.

Acknowledgements

Altogether, about half of the poems in this little collection were first published in journals both well known and obscure, in the U.S., England, and Australia. I wish I'd kept better track of them so I could properly credit and thank them.

According to one scrap of paper I found, the following poems first appeared elsewhere:

"Little Kohmeini" in 2AM; "A Tiger is Coming" in Brilliant Star; "Secrets" in Green Fuse; "Cheap Transportation" in Rocky Mt. Arsenal of the Arts; "Met Before" in Chattahoochee Review.

Another scrap of paper indicates that, during one year, some were published in the following journals. I don't know which poems went where: Alura, Confluent Education Journal, Ephemera, Elkhorn Review, Frugal Chariot, Gryphon, Golden Treasury of Great Poems, Ice River, Keyboard and Pen, The Lyric, Pangloss Papers, Poultry, Ransom, Resonance, ripples, Riverside Quarterly, Rocky Mountain Oyster, River Run, Wide Open, Writer's Haven.

Colorado poet Art Goodtimes once performed "Almost 39" in front of living humans. That may be the only time any of these have been given an audible voice.

Stones in the Water

Kenn Amdahl

www.ingramcontent.com/pod-product-compliance
Lightning Source LLC
Chambersburg PA
CBHW061334040426
42444CB00011B/2920